DOLLS

D1157744

CLAIRE MILLIKIN

DOLLS

POEMS

2LEAF PRESS

FLORIDA | NEW YORK

www.2leafpress.org

P.O. Box 4378
Grand Central Station
New York, New York 10163-4378
editor@2leafpress.org
www.2leafpress.org

2LEAF PRESS INC. is a Florida-based
nonprofit 501(c)(3) organization that promotes
multicultural literature and literacy.
www.2lpinc.org

Copyright © Claire Millikin Raymond 2021

Cover art: Broken Doll Face and
Head on Black Background © shellystill/stock.adobe.com

Book design and layout: Gabrielle David

Library of Congress Control Number: 2020951825

ISBN-13: 978-1-7346181-7-4 (Paperback)

10   9   8   7   6   5   4   3   2   1

Published in the United States of America

2Leaf Press trade distribution is handled by University of Chicago Press / Chicago Distribution Center (www.press.uchicago.edu) 773.702.7010. Titles are also available for corporate, premium, and special sales. Please direct inquiries to the UCP Sales Department, 773.702.7248.

All rights reserved. No part of this publication may be reproduced, stored in a retrieval system, or transmitted in any form or by any means electronic, mechanical, photocopied, recorded or otherwise without written permission from 2Leaf Press, Inc., except in the case of brief quotations embodied in critical reviews and certain other noncommercial uses permitted by copyright law. For permission requests, contact the publisher at editor@2leafpress.org.

For the memory of Sage Smith.

P O E M S

PREFACE vii

INTRODUCTION 1

PRIZEWINNERS OF THE APOCALYPSE 9

Prizewinners of the Apocalypse 11

Seven Stops 13

Doll Collectors 14

Dolls, Pure Formalities 15

The Mannequins 16

The Unpopular Dress 18

Floyd Burroughs' Cigarettes 19

Paper Doll Eyes 20

Baby Alive 21

Linear A and B 23

Floyd Burroughs' Second Pack of Cigarettes 24

Elegy for Sage Smith 25

Dolls of Tifton, Georgia 27

The Golden Thread 28

MEDICINE 31

Medicine for Broken Dolls 33

Anorexic Girl 34

Shopping Mall Dolls 35

Rooms Before Television 36

Pierced Dolls 37

Coke-bottle Barbie-doll 38

Evening Interior with Doll 40

Shoe-Box Doll House 41

Fugitive Summer Dolls 42

Lost Doll 43

Via Negativa 44

Train Doll 45

Mermaid T-Shirt 46

PHOTOGRAPHS 49

Selfie as Illusory Child at Birthday Party 51

Vesture 52

Shoes in Photographs 53

August Sander's "Man with
Dancing Bear, 1928, Westerwald" 54

Amatorium 55

Hans Bellmer's Dolls 56

Sister Shoe 57

Damaged Child 59

Escalator 60

Sacrificial Dolls 61

Claude Cahun 62

Fire 63

Salad Bar 64

Figurine 65

The Candle-Maker's Daughters 66

The Hunt 67

Rock, Paper, Scissors 69

Ephebus 71

Witness 72

Pretty Little Dolls 73

Photographs of Daughters 74

Carnal 75

Doll Photographer 77

HUMAN 79

What Little Girls Learn 81

Anatomically Correct.. 82

Movies About Solitary
Confinement 83

After Ballet 84

House for Book 85

Some Dolls 86

Cupboard.. 87

Union Station, Washington, D.C. 88

Rust.. 89

Princess Bed 90

Princess Coat... 91

Childhood Plays.. 92

Hostel Girls 93

Cloister... 94

The Doll I Was... 95

Night Insects 96

Action Figure Toys.. 97

Superhero Costume,
Attic, Tifton, Georgia... 99

Becoming a Doll 101

Peacock Coat...102

The Insect Doll 103

The Incest Doll 104

Manikin 105

Antique Doll.. 106

Doll Daughter.. 107

Growing Up Skipper 108

Dress Like A Girl.. 109

City of Disappeared Girls 110

The Puppet King.. 112

Doll Mother 114

Rabbit Theory 115

Bright Shoes.. 117

ABOUT THE POET 121

OTHER BOOKS BY 2LEAF PRESS 123

PREFACE

SAGE SMITH DISAPPEARED from Charlottesville in November 2012. She was a young Black transwoman, delicately built, with an expressive and pretty face. Her disappearance fell between the much more well-known disappearances of Morgan Harrington and Hannah Graham, who were White, blonde, college students, about the same age as Sage at the time of their disappearance. Morgan and Hannah's bodies were found through intense searching, but Sage remains missing, presumed dead. Significantly less man-power and public attention, for whatever reasons, very possibly for reasons having to do with racism and transphobia, were given to finding Sage as compared with the searches for Morgan and Hannah. Sage remains un-found, undiscovered. Her family continues to mourn her, but her city has, in that terrible phrase, moved on. My book of poems, *Dolls*, is dedicated to the memory of Sage Smith because in her beauty, her femininity, and in the erasure or rather near-erasure, of her presence from her hometown, Charlottesville, she emblematizes the themes of this book: the conscription of femininity to suffering in the traditional South.

How is it that a middle-aged White ciswoman comes to write about a young Black transwoman? This book, *Dolls,* like all my books of poetry, emerges through a process like a haunting. It is not that Sage is a ghost but that she acts like a ghost in my mind. How do we speak for the silenced? That is the question that *Dolls* asks. Sage cannot, now, speak for herself. But she is on record as having said, of her transition, "Respect it!" and that is the key-note of this poetry collection. Respect for precisely those who have received too little or none of it. Respect Sage Smith, yes. Respect what it means to live through, live in, live on, with the deathliness of racism and sexism as if you were a doll. Femininity is translated into a brutal system of constriction in the South. As a child and as a younger woman, I was seen as pretty, which meant being treated differently, like a doll. Not only did I survive childhood sexual abuse, but even as I "outgrew" that category, the violence of being seen as the femme continued. It marked me. Even now, when I am middle-aged and no longer pretty, in that way, my life contracts around the nodus of being seen and the need to evade the brunt of that kind of haunted visibility.

Sage, in her hyper-visible invisibility, is a double-figure. On the streets of Charlottesville, the pretty, Black transwoman stood out. She looked different from the manicured, well-to-do White femmes who are the norm in the South. In this, she was hyper-visible, vulnerable to attack. She lacked the implicit cultural supports that typically attend wealthy White girls, and in this lack of support, Sage was invisible. In her disappearance, she became again hyper-visible—known to the media—and invisible—no longer seen in Charlottesville. The doll's lot is both hyper-visible, an object for seeing, and invisible, an object the eye glances beyond. The poems of Dolls encounter the doll, moving in deep to lay bare what it is we do to feminine people in the South and how race cuts us apart. Here, in the plague winter of December 2020, having been newly fired after fifteen years of teaching at the University of Virginia, I thought I would be long gone from Charlottesville, but am held here by an unwillingness to risk the travel to establish a new domicile while Donald Trump's egregious policies foment a catastrophic rise in COVID-19 cases in the United States. So it is, maybe fittingly, from Charlottesville that I complete the editing of the Dolls and write this preface, in mourning for Charlottesville native Sage Smith. And it is in hope, as hope is part of every venture of language, every step of *poesis,* that for those who read my words, Sage is a figure given honor. And in the hope that for those who read my words, the violence of Southern femininity is lifted, however slowly, through language's ability to pull apart and make new the weft of the human world. ∎

—Claire Millikin
Charlottesville, Virginia
December 2020

INTRODUCTION

SOME READERS MIGHT OVERLOOK the dedication page of a book thinking it might be too elusive to comprehend without proper context. A dedication page can be humorous, witty, or somber in tone, and can be directed toward a particular person or group of people, and it can offer a fascinating glance into an author's life and times. Many celebrated writers such as James Baldwin, Toni Morrison, and Marilyn Nelson have used the dedication page to make profound historical, political, and social statements. It is in this very tradition that Claire Millikin's dedication page to her eighth book of poetry, *Dolls,* functions by offering a deeply moving sincerity as it solemnly reads: "For the memory of Sage Smith." While many readers might not initially be aware of the still unsolved 2012 disappearance of Sage Smith, a nineteen-year-old Black transwoman from Charlottesville, Virginia, the images, themes, and sentiments expressed in Millikin's *Dolls* act as fervent poetic orisons that ask of readers not to disregard the lives of those who have been, and continue to be, silenced.

Millikin writes in her Preface, "This book, *Dolls,* like all my books of poetry, emerges through a process like a haunting" (viii). For some, the word "haunting" tends to hold an eerie connotation, that of a seemingly "disruptive" singular spirit, or multiple spirits, standing persistently at the threshold of the earthly and the otherworldly. One can see that for a gifted and highly skilled poet like Millikin, this "haunting" experience was contemplative, enriching, and inspirational, and at times maddening, hurtful, and traumatic. These complex emotions are powerfully expressed throughout *Dolls* allowing a reader to confront the ways in which discussions of the intersections of gender, gender expression and identity, race, socio-economic status, sexuality, and sexual orientation are prevalent in 21st century U.S. American society.

Dolls is masterfully divided into four sections offering poems that invite a reader to become immersed in the speaker's perceptive observations on a variety of subjects. Millikin's opening poem "Prizewinners of the Apocalypse," is written in the first-person perspective as a means of adding her own personal testimony about the two-day white supremacist rally held in Charlottesville, Virginia in August 2017. The first stanza reads:

> Men entered my city bearing torches, chanting vengeance,
> for acts no one had committed against them.
> Carrying torches, men circled statues of Confederate generals.
> I wanted to find human ground,
> but the town was the only town where I lived.

These five lines are one of the many instances in Millikin's collection in which a reader takes on the vantage point of a seemingly silent and stationary, open-eyed doll. The emphatic use of the "I" acts as the life-force of Millikin's collection. How does one "find human ground" when anger, misunderstanding and eminent danger is so close to one's doorstep? There's no simple answer to this essential question and while the speaker feels paralyzed, the impulse to craft a poem takes hold of the speaker amidst the turmoil. In the final couplet of the poem, the speaker directly addresses Sage Smith in a woeful tone of voice, "And you are gone, Sage Smith, / vanished. Your city *bereft*" (12, emphasis added), signaling how palpable her presence will be throughout the collection.

In another poem titled "Dolls of Tifton, Georgia" the speaker recounts a doll shopping trip with her grandmother when she was a child. The dolls are showcased in the drugstore windows in the most flattering of ways to entice a young girl. It's a poem that invites the reader to consider the intricate social trappings of how a young girl should behave and present herself before others, especially her grandmother: "I want to take home the prize— / the doll that looks like her idea of a good child." In these lines, one sees the ways in which the young girl, and the coveted "good" doll, is at odds with one another since the doll will never grow into a young woman having to face a brutally sexist and superficial society that conscripts femininity to a battery of impossible-to-achieve rules and regulations.

The section titled "Photographs," features a series of ekphrastic poems based on the art, photography and lives of American and European artists such as Hans Bellmer, Claude Cahun (Lucy Schwob), Dorothea Lange and August Sander. In the poem titled "Claude Cahun," inspired by the early twentieth century French Surrealist photographer who was known for her self-portraits that explored gender identity, the speaker ponders about the many masks one must wear to conform to cultural and societal expectations of gender roles. These poems invite the reader to research these artists' works and to think critically and creatively about visual representation and the ways in which their artistic statements resonate.

Each poem in Claire Millikin's *Dolls* carries a rhythmic pulse, like the beating of a restless drum, demanding to be heard against the damaging structures of gendered and racial oppression. ∎

—Sean Frederick Forbes
Thompson, Connecticut
July 2021

The world that opens and shuts,
like the eye of the wax doll.

—Emily Dickinson

PRIZEWINNERS OF
THE APOCALYPSE

Prizewinners of the Apocalypse

Men entered my city bearing torches, chanting vengeance,
for acts no one had committed against them.
Carrying torches they circled statues of Confederate generals.
I wanted to find human ground,
but the town was the only town where I lived.

Men entered my country carrying slogans,
hating anyone whose skin wasn't pale,
marching as they vowed to *save* America.
I wasn't sure what America is, or was.
But I knew they were saving no one.
I slept fitfully, always ready to run
if they converged on my own door
noticing my language wasn't theirs.

I wanted to find a place to be calm
but my country was the only country where I was born,
the house the only house I own,
walls fraying in disrepair, yard tugged by forest's feral animals.

In my country, they locked children in hard rooms
to save what they called the law. I know
what they did to those children
and it will never heal.
But my country is my country still
so I will vote them out.

Early morning dreams, I see these slender horses,
translucent, the color of dawn sky
flickering and wavering
and I don't know what is coming
but I know the prize
of the apocalypse varies according
to which book you read, which deity you worship.

And you are gone, Sage Smith,
vanished. Your city bereft.

Seven Stops

after Joseph Cornell's *7 Tears of Saint Lucia*

The tears of Saint Lucy rattle me.
That she was given the choice to lose either her eyes or her soul,
and kept her soul. Where I'd choose vision,
seeing all the way through.

Joseph Cornell doesn't give it away.
Seven tears, blue stones.

Saint Lucia, I'm alert to your problem:
It's not unlike my own. From French,
translate back to the Italian,
to the mother's lucid voice, or the ocean's.
Translated, clearly, our names mean *light*

without tremolo, the purest line.
Wanting an original document of blue fields at dusk,
I bought Nina Simone's albums to play for my son
before he was born. I'd lean
my pregnant belly close to the speaker,

for him to hear with new ears.
With her baroque emotions,
mother kept silent in the long days
of my infancy. No wonder I cry glass tears.
Lithic stars, lacquer box, the name

        means light in every translation. Ride
my bike farther into fields.
Seven stops.

Doll Collectors

A doll never complains. A doll's voice
is a false-front, a pretense,
like the idea of American happiness,

that is only for the wealthy.
Shadowing backyard pear trees, moths
press an almost human sigh.

The dead cannot ask the living
for grace. It goes the other way.
Hence, doll collectors fill shelves

in houses of oblique mourning,
never saving
for whom they suppress their tears.

Dolls, Pure Formalities

Formal, only as form they persist,
shadow's lineament. Lost or found,
doesn't count in the tesseract fold
of the risen Christ, some believe,
but I'm stalled at the bend.

Afterimages of dolls in shopping malls haunted me
as a child: How did they breathe?
The aunts wept and prayed
but salvation left me alone.
Only the taste of mother's fingers
across my lips sounded love,

hush, don't ask
so many questions.

The Mannequins

Nothing that surrounds us is object, all is subject.
—André Breton

Suffer from chronic insomnia,
wracked by half-waking dreams.
How could it be otherwise?
Holding always the same posture,
same half-smile, slight tilt of gaze.

At store windows, the world stalls.
The mannequin's shadow, perfect and bereft,
falls across us. I never left
school but stayed, carrying
a secret that that only I atone.

Tobacco rises in fields, a golden plinth for sky.
This is where I'm from,
I belong here, but my hands are tied.
The stillness of sleep
attends them, but never sleep itself;

less than statues, painted molds.
At last I will put them on,
garments of the mannequin,
vestments of uneasy summer morning
when heat rises through pinewoods corrugating rough.

Hold still, brace for summer's aftermath.
As a small child, I believed
mannequins kinder than my father,
and cleaved to their hands, unwilling
to be taken from the store.

The Unpopular Dress

It hurt to wear it, too tight for easy breath.
And I knew the anguish would last
hours after I took it off. But the way it made me look.
That was lethal.

Pupal, like emerging from the larval stage peel it off
red rim by rim, wing
on wing, the darkness of translation.
In a photograph, the unloved dress
outshines time itself, not waiting
but transfigured
tarnish of another's mirror.

The pain of flesh
is mathematical, according to vertices.
Pupal, inside the carapace of dress,
I metamorphosed into something more and less.
I've always disliked the way that I look
but most of life is surface.

Unpopular at best, it's hated now. Red dress, call back
to the past and you get an empty closet
with the mirror
of your mother's face, still haunted
by how she never saved you
and never tried to.

Floyd Burroughs' Cigarettes

Searching for my daughter
among the world's lost metaphors,
I saw Walker Evans' photograph
of a shack in western Alabama. 1936.

Driving that country still terrifies me,
because it's home.
When Walker snapped the shot,
Floyd had just stopped reaching

into his pocket for cigarettes, unfiltered,
the kind that singe your voice, every word.
I was searching for my daughter
among the vanished curls and tendrils of this universe.

I was searching in the smoke
that is the breath of men.
Cigarettes are not dishonest objects,
they do what they claim: make your voice

visible in the night sky, burn your words.
In western Georgia, at the Alabama border, we played
tag with our cars, riding time.
Without smoke, without mirrors

lens, cinder, distance.
He reaches into his pocket
for the stash, tobacco. No daughter
from that distant west walks back.

Paper Doll Eyes

The violent side of paper dolls cannot be entirely disguised,
eviscerated bodies, without depth. Mirrors inadequately twin them.

Deserts of light, salterns where salt dries
in ascending pools. Sky's corrosive tears, the paper doll's eye holds.

Cut along dotted lines, bruised by shadow,
what do they see, so framed,
like the church sextant, to be

in the holy place but not be holy?
A desert of light, paper doll eyes,
trompe l'oeil. Masks of vision or maybe just nothing.

In winter, I painted the room
so that nothing remained of his voice,
purchased thick pale paint, coated walls with it.

Dusk when I was done, lacquer sky slaking down the elms.
Paper dolls are made to be torn,
too fragile to evade harm for long.

Baby Alive

The doll's hands curled on nothing, our neighborhood gone
when Julie-Christine's father moved west of town,
planting gladioli in new fields.
For verisimilitude, recall *Baby Alive* of 1979.

This doll we shared, *Baby Alive* swallowed an eerie substance
that looked like milk and smelled of banana,
then wet its diaper with a scent of plastic and sugar.
In childhood's hypogeal lands, watching soap operas
while her mother's pills wore off,
we'd pass the vivid doll between us.

One bright afternoon, I noted: *The only way to prove
she's alive is see if she can die.*
Hitched the doll on my hip, climbed
the great oak on the western ridge
higher than before, shimmying
in my Sunday dress toward heaven.

The absence of houses all around
made the world look new, like a story
never told, so you can end it
any way you choose. Standing below,
Julie Christine cried, *do it!* I loosed
the plastic infant from my hands. Quick

as breath, wanted to catch it back,
but *Baby Alive* plummeted, vested

by gravity, drag of sky, flickering oak
branches met in descent. Irrevocably,
she fell, hitting at last where root-

flare echoed leaf canopy,
and the engine of her shut. I saw
her then neither subject nor object,
but something else, like in bad dreams
when you speak strangely,
between language and a cry.

Linear A and B

A paper doll is cousin to the leaf, though human in form.
Folios of unspeakable sorrow, where the town becomes only a road.

Their eyes daubs, fingers maimed in the process of cutting.
For what they see cannot be codified but only felt,

outlines of roughly torn glorioles.
Dogwood blossoms in the backyard fray,

algebraic wreckage. Infinitely many solutions to the line,
but paper dolls are cut as they are cut.

Floyd Burroughs' Second Pack of Cigarettes

In his left front pocket, calculators
of breath. Tobacco, a gift crop
in my childhood country. One more gift
I squandered to survive.

In the eastern light of strangers' cars
catch my reflection by that glass, glint of flesh.
I'm looking for an aperture
through which to divide myself. Get past this.

A thousand miles north from Georgia
he said, *I'll give you a ride girl.*
A cigarette is an offering.
It turns your voice to smoke

to be swallowed by God or sky.
After the photographer left
Floyd definitely lit up a new cigarette
and, smoking it, came back to himself,

which is all I want—
back to that still place, the name I never gave her.

Elegy for Sage Smith

Trace the dark schedule
with fingers beringed. *Sage Smith last seen*
at the Charlottesville train station, 8.30 at night,

November 20th. Checking departures, arrivals,
rehearse the ways you might escape
at the outskirts, daughter, the outskirts

where the station offers its premise of flight.
A train route tracks a kind of infinity:
it circles and comes back, always to the same stops.

Morning finds your bed empty. The police give up too early.
As if you belonged to no one.
But you belong here. This *is* your city.

A train can take a passenger anywhere by land,
provided they've patience for the distance.
Trace variant routes, fingers in glinting rings.

November sky mimes heaven, universe, whatever
vermilion myth flies.
Five years later, your grandmother still searches

for someone to listen. Those professors who paid
for your visits didn't save you. They didn't try.
How far the outskirts reach. Vespers

freeze early winter's backyards. Vector
fields map equations
that leave out poor black girls

born male in Charlottesville.
A shelfless night, now, a lacquer box of partitions.
This always unfixed departure date.

Dolls of Tifton, Georgia

Afternoon's navy sky reflects
grandmother's face and mine, leaning
close to sealed drugstore windows
showcasing dolls. Pale vinyl

dolls, salt-blue eyes and rust lips.
Their silence is from everlasting.
I want to take home the prize—
the doll that looks like her idea of a good child.

Deep beneath sky, cotton fields slip
into red earth, rags of longing.
I'm more afraid of the color blue, cobalt,
meridian hitch, than of darkness. On the hot

sidewalk, we stand before glass,
dolls staring through us. If the day is a forsaken room
dolls hold it still, so still, the infinite noun in their mouths.
Grandmother has enough money to buy, but not enough

to not feel the purchase. Their reflected faces
merge with our faces in the glass, our bodies theirs, nothing
but image, mystic windows. Girls who give up everything
to have nothing, to *really* have it.

Nothing but lost places on the sidewalk in Tifton,
Georgia, emptying before rainstorm.
Little doll, stony diatom. At fields' outskirts,
streets ravel into cotton's hair-like plants.

The Golden Thread

Karina is stitching my hands with a golden thread.
She works carefully following a pattern from her mind's eye.
Each stitch draws blood. At last I tell her it hurts too much, stop.
She stops immediately but the wounds stay, the thread deeply lodged.

She is stitching my hands with the golden thread.
We are in her mother's kitchen after the service
of Christian burial, and at evening the food's all gone
only wine is left, which I don't drink
but she's drunk a lot, beyond communion.

And she begins to stitch my hands so seriously, intently
without asking, an act of care, devotion
determination. We sit together in the darkening kitchen
after they bury her mother, in the hard sunlight of early summer
that fills the pine trees and hickory with golden threads

catching the forest to the house, esemplastic,
making the forest part of the house, the kitchen still full
of her mother's teas and sugars, her mother's shoes at the door,
her mother's rugs, carried from Karachi, daughter of Barbarikon.
And from the seamstress' closet, she chooses

the golden thread to stitch my hands,
and I hold still as the needle moves deep enough
into the flesh to anchor the thread, to set the pattern
that she draws, the pattern I write now,
midsummer, the sun at that height that pierces.

MEDICINE

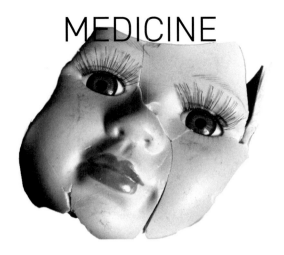

She stares into space like a china doll.
—Elliott Smith, *Waltz 2*

Medicine for Broken Dolls

Glue the snapped finger,
tape the cracked nape of neck,
tug stitching along a torn hem.
What's left is something less.

 Though we mend and name them,
they won't approach our balm. Dolls
take over any room in which they're set—
on shelves, chairs, eerie in cribs,

 turnstiles for their immaterial sleep—
they alter space
with unseeing gaze. Once reft,
how to knit back the frayed seam

 of bad dreams? Or trace back
spring's tattered weather, fan
of dogwood, dehiscent
bruise in the center of bloom.

Grandfather takes me for lunch at the café
in the center of Montgomery, Alabama,
spring light filling trees bright as pain.

He'd say *get anything you want,*
and call me by my real name,
the one inherited through him.

It's how old men prepare for death:
Tell a granddaughter, here is your name.
You can survive this.

Anorexic Girl

I got curious about the etymology of girl.
It did not always mean female—
originally *girl* meant *small, ignorant,*
lacking heft, intellect. Some philologists
say that *girl* once connoted

worthlessness, any living creature
considered weak, whether human or animal.
Others wager the word's source more obscure.
No one knows the first time
a human girl decided to starve herself,

go further toward the vanishing
people want from her.
The penance of fasting, taken up
by those longing to be saints and the word *girl*
emerge at about the same time and place: Medieval

Europe. Starving yourself is old
hat, it goes back, transcendent.
Along the lines of girl also, *call-girl, match-girl, girlie*.
Catch-words for the discardable.
Finally, at age 15,

after a year of boundless fasting, I stopped
starving myself. But it took decades
after that to lose the habit
of silence, hunger's match.

Shopping Mall Dolls

In derelict shopping malls, we shopped for dolls
like Evangelicals drag for souls.
Pack the car with the weight of rain,

drive part time 'til you get there,
the rest of your life this patience.
Sometimes the journey releases you, metic,

for salvation is a forest, at the edge
of which the battered equipment of childhood persists.
A man will say, *this is what I need from you,*

and the car drives for miles, for years, then it's done,
rusted chassis abandoned by train tracks.
Walk back through scrublands to parking lots,

retrieve the pieces. Object on object,
all can be translated to image
but never turned back to the place before touch. Strip

malls tremble in morning heat, managers tugging
their hearts into place. Purchase the stuff:
All New Materials, at full cost.

Rooms Before Television

In that early silence, it was easy to lose one's footing.

Precarious before television,
balance in front of blank time,
human voices like insects flickering
through breathing trees that crackle at the screen.

Rain began and feral animals
carried it on their backs from the forest.

We purchased a television set, then, an object
both hard and soft,
like an unmade bed, just after someone's left it.

From the side porch of great-aunt's house, I caught
elegy's peripheral glance.
It won't leave me.
Night sky can't turn back,
only cross America's highways, one after the next.

Pierced Dolls

Those places go down so much further in America,
you cannot imagine how deep,

crested by kestrel, merlin,
the small bitter hawks of grief.

A swallow in the house some say means death, even so
shadows of birds crossing
a road off the Interstate bruise the ground.

In doll houses, one wall's always open,
so anyone can reach in.

Maybe Christ *was* pierced five times, opened to endless night
as over the broken

bodies of homeless men millions step with averted eyes.
So much deeper than America, these roads leading nowhere.

A dollhouse is a fragile bone,
furcula, what you might wish for.

Coke-bottle Barbie-doll

Step the ghosts in relict summer light,
for in the big house lived great-aunt
with her lifelong companion, a woman
they politely called her servant, Georgia.
Georgia once showed me, the smallest daughter,

Southern-belle Barbie-dolls she'd fashioned
from wide plastic Coke bottles cut in half,
shaping soundless bells.
She'd amputate the Barbie's legs, soldering
with airplane glue the doll's torso
to the Coke bottle's slender mouth.

Miserere, polyethylene bells, intricate crotchet
she stitched gowns of white and gold—
cascade bodice, plume of skirt, spilled
appanage of petals, a row of dolls
so hemmed you'd cry to touch,
being a child of nine.

Belles on shelves shadowed the blue veranda.
The two women never took it outside.
As the porch fan turned its winking eye
she allowed me, only a child,
to cradle her creations—Barbies amputated
from the waist down, conjoined with Coke
bottle halves, lining the side porch,

floor and ceiling painted water blue
to keep out ghosts. When great-aunt died,
Georgia moved back to her people, in Alma.
And our family sold the house to a Bed & Breakfast,
bells of August sounding
from all the town-square churches.

Evening Interior with Doll

There's no real use for dolls.
Even so, handed a doll
the holder becomes somewhat magical,
albeit in a lost kind of way.

When I was a child,
Grandmother bought for me a dark-skinned doll
with black hair and sharp eyes,
like my mother's, and grandmother's,

and kept it hidden in the sewing room.
A moral form a doll holds—
standing in judgment. A few years
after that doll, I learned to cross the road

with boys saying, *Come on*
this will be a great party
and it's dusk, our coats like animal pelts
shine, immaculate. A doll

fills the space in which she is set.
In that room, you really cannot look
at anything else.

Shoe-Box Doll House

At age thirteen, I built a dollhouse in my narrow closet.
Room on room of discarded shoeboxes,
pristine Mondrian squares
connected by the extreme logic
of filial trash. *Meditatio,*

Body of Christ, Bread of salvation.

The house had no doorways
but of each box a fourth wall was missing, an open wound.
Décor of left-over wrapping paper, glitzy tinsel,
house stacked ten stories high, three wide,
a foyer making it thirty-one

shoe-box rooms, with no inhabitants.
Meditatio, tell the priest your baptismal name,

Forehead of Christ, Wrist of salvation.

In the borrowed yard of that year's rental,
grass darkened with neglect, virid and lush.
As spring came on, I stopped
eating anything but apples. Only three apples each day,
standing for hours before the shoe-box house,

staring, cradling
a stripped core in my hands.

Fugitive Summer Dolls

Dolls have a human form, but no human needs.
Scattered light will shiver,
glancing through space. Dolls don't dream.

Fugitive August light on damp grass, glinting
with small dents of sky
as if someone spread sugar across the blades.

In dreams, my mother tells me she cannot confess
what she's seen him do to me,
too horrible to say it aloud.

The homeless often wait, surrounded by plastic bags
like minions, patient in bus stations, imagining
tickets for some as yet unspoken destination.

Lost Doll

Remember the lost one? Left on a playground,
dropped at dusk, rushing home for supper.

Abandoned beneath the swing-set, another pair of hands
take her up. Just so, I left the world

of Creative Writing because a guy in my workshop started
writing prose poems, short-shorts, about me,

including my Christian name. He brought them into workshop
where the professor critiqued

his use of metaphor. Other students tittered
while the guy had sex with me

in the lines of his writing.
I raised my hand but was never called on.

My name, however, was spoken.
In New Haven, at the turn

of the century, a feral dog
circled the gated college. We were waiting all night, drunk

out of our minds, as snow fell
like broken glass, but rounder, in softened shards.

As if you could be broken and not feel it.
Become whole again, that lost doll in your hands.

Via Negativa

Dolls hold a negative fascination.
They can never do what they want,
every act happens by someone else's touch.

Only violence changes them,
as their wounds that cannot be healed, just taped over.

At the bus stop, she's carrying a doll so realistic
it looks like a human infant. Except no voice.
Finite and infinite,

the doll's beauty is like that of insects
seen closely in bad dreams.

Too many motels I've stayed in, trying
to find sleep like a lost language,
a submerged mother-tongue.

At the motel sink, wash my face.

On the back wall, left by accident, a robe
sized for a boy of eight years,
decorated with superheroes,
their fists poised like roses.

Train Doll

In the house, mother divided the rooms
into before and after. But that line never holds.

How I longed to be like her, unfeeling,
folding her cold body to my body across the miles.

She was a symptom not a cure:
blonde hair and round blue eyes, thin lips. Her face entirely
unlike mine.

On trains, I kept the doll close, the one object I owned.
Train tracks laid a century back will crack under high speeds.

Traveling too far
into yourself can cause permanent harm.

Dolls speak either no language or a too private psalm.
When first they constructed the rail lines, it was impossible

for those in neighboring houses to sleep. Then the sound became
familiar.
You get used to anything, they say.

Maybe I learned languages too quickly, not catching the subtexts.
Doll of my fate,

which being translated means
ride the train now, go anywhere but here.

Mermaid T-Shirt

When you're in it, the ocean sounds metallic,
a benthic drum. It tastes
like blood, biting your tongue.
She's wearing a mermaid T-shirt,
crouched where light pools pelagic. Woman
in a child's garment,

lifting books, one by one,
return the fallen to order, lectic,
her legs seamless in dark jeans, a mermaid's curve,
matching the T-shirt she's kept
stretching and mending
all the years since her mother left.

PHOTOGRAPHS

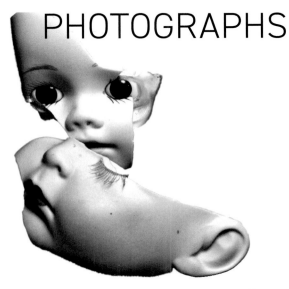

In order to see a photograph well, it is best to look away.

—Roland Barthes

Selfie as Illusory Child at Birthday Party

The reasons for betrayal are always unfair.
Uneasy with false cheer, mother combed my hair
after whipping me, saying, *don't cry,*
it's unbecoming to a young lady.
A room filled with amaryllis, darkened by shadow.

Childhood is real but also fake, like purple skies
layering variegated shadows.
In shadow, amaryllis looks like hyacinth.
Or maybe they're the same?
If I were diligent, I'd look it up
but I've got no stamina,
having been too often whipped.

Cold rainstorm made it urgent that we stay
in the rented house, room heavy with rain
shadows and pine trees
reflecting inwards through glass skies.
I do not speak in psalm but in elegy.

A room is not holy
until someone tells the truth there
but the truth is uneasy, a kind of raw ecstasy.
Pine branches rake against glass,
advice I should never have taken,
hearing in the rain my mother's warning
don't cry, it's unbecoming.

For my birthday I wore a sea-blue
horizon, a line in the mind.

Vesture

Bought the dress back, year by year,
on installment plan.

A voice after menarche could be butterfly or ruler

but misses these realms by a letter.
Golden oaks shed in November, rich dresses unfurled.

Don't ask your sisters to care,
only wear the dress.

Shoes in Photographs

In the post-office line,
I intend to wait until I hear the reason
the woman who stands asking
Did my brother send that money order?

always gets the same cold shoulder.
Integration by parts
stretches equations toward zero or infinity.
My shoes, marked with crossing,

draw the dirt of fields into this story.
With her letters, mother returns
a photograph of me holding that doll
in kindergarten, the one I loved for its pinafore,

the letter also asking why I never made good.

August Sander's "Man with Dancing Bear, 1928, Westerwald"

That frozen morning, a man holds a bear on a chain
that also encircles the man's torso.
The man might be Roma, traveling the Westerwald
with his dancing bear, seeking a little food, a place to sleep.
For centuries, Roma trained bears to perform

in Europe, a way to survive. In the war,
Nazis put Romani in concentration camps
and the bears they put into the Frankfurt zoo.
After the bombing of the Frankfurt zoo,
surviving bears got transported to zoos in the provinces

and in those zoos starved, dying also of winter exposure,
as the war took everything with nothing left over.
These frozen mornings, I think of the dancing bear.
The hard part for the bear surely was the dance, standing for
so long
on hind legs. Maybe he loved the man who fed him,

or held an animal grief,
unable to recall the time before captivity.
Or maybe in the memory of the bear is all history
unfolding in an instant, *Angelus Novus,* a bear or a God,
carrying the psalm of last chances, too many

have been forced to speak
silently to themselves.

Amatorium

During the pandemic it came out that half my friends
were involved in extramarital affairs.
Panicked over whether to shelter in place with their spouses
or lovers. I don't have many friends,
so it's not a representative sample. But still.

In the absence of pesticides, and during the season of heavy rains,
insects swarmed and the water in the aquifer grew pure.
So pure that at last I could drink from it
swallowing down to that holy dark
from which dreams of cold clarity emerge.

The South holds America hostage.
I am a Southerner by birth, and what else is our history?
Studying the history of Georgia, I stumbled
onto an 18th century ancestor, one Robert Goudy,
who lived among the Creek and Cherokee, cheating them, and
raping them,

which he called marriage, several "wives" at his disposal.
My father is suffering this summer, an old man with cancer.
Should I forgive his love for me?
I keep the lens of vision open, a shallow depth of field.

Hans Bellmer's Dolls

It can feel like being torn apart
to look at his photographs.
You touch your fingers
to your elbows, surprised
by the integument of your own body.

Relative to light, time and space dilate.
But the body keeps one pace
moving toward a final beat.
Bellmer's dolls are disturbing, human forms

all torn up. Looks to me like he was a real creep.
And yet the voices of those who take
you apart are often the gentlest,
full of care and watchfulness.

I'm faithful now only to the distances
within words, lengths
inside names, anagrams, apostrophes.
His photographs of dolls return to that story

of autumn and the camera.
The world going up in smoke.

Sister Shoe

i.
She tells me *play the music*
they played when they hurt her.
She wants to hear it in a new light.

Or maybe it's the only music that is real for her.

don't wear your sister's shoes he'd say,
but I'm already related to her
unspeakable grief.

In the transit work of shoes, step
by tonal shift, slap arpeggio, psaltic grift.
Carry us past what's been done

in the names of nations.

I am a mirror of another sort.
Haunted by different music.

ii.
That's probably why she reached for me
Play that music; I know you know it.

Hold my hand, find a way through the notes.

iii.
Which regime ruins you,
that's the music you listen to,
trying to understand, the shame of it.

iv.
I was named for Sarah, for Sarah,
back down the line, two hundred years
to the first, in Georgia, who had no choice.

Damaged Child

after the Dorothea Lange photograph

Lange's camera caught the child at an edge
of Oklahoma farm. Nothing moves

in that picture; but somehow the child's hands
seem to open and open toward us, like saints' hands
in frayed paintings, in Sunday school classrooms

when you've stared too long. Name the beasts,
angels, and devils, side by side, who survives,

who gets sacrificed. Scrub pine
and petiolated live oak, look
past this country.

Escalator

Going down feels scary but don't worry,
the long shadow of gravity
hardly touches amid plastic greenery,
as the machine shakes in steel traverse,

a shining slant descent.
At age 3, my doll got caught
in escalator stairs' interlocking teeth.
I fought but couldn't wrest it free.

The whole works jolted to a choke.
A woman standing behind me screamed *baby, baby*
in Cantonese. We lived
in Singapore then. The word rang *baby!*

Strong hands lifted me.
It wasn't the doll, I was the baby
they were saving as the escalator hitched,
wrenching the doll in its shift.

Heavy metal, lead draws all things downward,
the way a sky shuts with rain.
Escalator pulling endlessly to its one destination
of parking garage mirrors.

Sacrificial Dolls

Interviewed fifty years later, she confessed
she submitted to the surgery to hold onto welfare.
Survivor, telling her story on a Sunday night
television special. She never wept,

just showed the interviewer her collection of dolls,
explaining that none was damaged.
In North Carolina, thousands like her
got sterilized by state mandate.

Her line of work wasn't revealed in the interview,
but she'd earned enough to buy
porcelain dolls, set in several rows, painted, pristine objects.
Slowly the camera panned across the dolls, the woman's voice

continuing its story. Doll: Impassive, relict suffering.
The dolls stood beside and behind
the speaker, once a victim. A common wound
dolls carry, shocked messengers,

their expressions always of disdain.
Even when smiling, a doll looks askance,
judging what was done in the name of science.
I went to high school in North Carolina,

got solitary for a few months in treatment
for juvenile truants.
My camera is language.
The story dreams me still.

Claude Cahun

Beneath each mask, another mask,
for objects cannot be torn from shadows.
In darkness, boundaries melt.
But photographs require light.
I will never finish taking off all my masks.

Auto-portrait: In the thick Edwardian cabinet
inherited from your father, you curl,
a doll, a proffered gift.
Dolls are close to the dead, also photographs.
Your camera a bow and arrow, yourself the target.

Lately I think I should do it—
dye my hair, fake it a few more years,
transfigure time's wear. Leave this job.
You never put up with it. Never tried for a man's eye,
or hustled for the buck.

Posing in your father's cupboard as a doll,
as your beloved Suzanne/Marcel snapped the shot,
you froze, still as death.
Maybe you shook with laughter, after?
Or maybe it was all too real. Did you ever escape?

Hiding from Nazis on the Isle of Jersey, secreted
in a box beneath the bed, decades of *auto-portraits.*
Lungs trashed by that fascist prison, you left
self-portrait photographs. Mask after mask after mask.
Doll-selves of paper and light. Lucy Schwob.

Fire

Down by the river after rain, gather sticks
for a wet fire, sparks
that will shatter the room with light.

Into the river in winter folds an unwashed snow.
He's twenty-six, I'm thirteen.
Doll he chooses, everyone knows why.

Closet of precipitate, condensed mirror,
I no longer love you
if ever I did.

Salad Bar

Girls aren't seen as children in my family of origin
but miniature wives. Even so
I went to college, a work-study job in the dining hall.
My shift was "Salad 2," not creating the salads,
just stand at the salad bar from six-til-eight p.m.,

catch all that has fallen – wipe up the dressing
its blue, orange, cream designs, pick up stray gray
leaves of lettuce, polish the stainless steel
with the same rag that feels dirty in hands,
but makes the metal gleam with elbow grease.

A young man from a family that bred horses,
a fellow student, visited me at the end of every shift,
evenings when light grafted through dying elms
filling the dining hall's corners and tables
with spent, useless gold. Scion,

he'd say, *right here, right on this table*
I'm ready for you, leering,
so I went red. That was surely what he wanted
to see how it was not funny to me. I wasn't embarrassed.
I hated him, hated the job. Never said a word.
It was how I learned to become a statue.

Figurine

From the abandoned orchard at the back of the road,
apple trees cast shadows along glass cabinetry
wherein rest porcelain figurines.

I can't do it anymore, hold that porcelain silence
of the figurine –

ankles, wrists,
figurine forms have no life, of course, but they have plenty
of history. These days of early summer

the light looks fragile
as if someone opened the door
into a room where I'm changing clothes

suddenly exposed,
this thin a shelf on which I'm set, a direct descendant
of figurines. Apple blossoms blown

inside through open windows,
look like fragments of the broken world.

The Candle-Maker's Daughters

Their flesh was wax, even so the girls competed
for smoothest, most translucent.
They didn't see until too late what winning brought,
how the very substance of which he'd made them
meant vanishing. Girls of wax, so perfect
in the initial aspect, don't last.

He never confessed what he'd done,
what men paid him. He was proud
of the works of his hands. Each girl desirable
for a night, a few weeks, maybe a year. No matter her collapsed

form afterwards, nothing
awaiting his daughters of wax.
He'd always intended that they burn.
If only one limped away, through a partly opened rain...
clutching herself to herself.

Cold shadows setting her
a new form. Her story to tell.

The Hunt

Only in television shows of the late
nineteen-seventies have I felt at home:
here the deer are unharmed
and the parents have names without known history,
Jimmy and Totsie.

I know, we all have a history,
every word a path through darkness,
but a word is also part of the darkness.

This morning talking with a man
whose wife died last spring,
I remember that only on television
do the dead return;

blur the line, the path that thaws, I'm wary
of early warmth, small flowers darkening
before rain. Who is faithful?

The television parents
never loved their children
actors hired by the studio
to play for laughs, looking nothing like them:

imagine the theater intact,
the man's wife alive
and I'm still fifteen years old, able to run seventy

miles per week without feeling it,
imagine the rain is no mirror
but only sky in time and light,

and Karina and I take the subway
sharing a coffee all the way
to the botanical gardens in the Bronx
to see the roses' new faces.
A bud is a kind of scar
that opens into starry difference

the small flowers darken with rain.

Rock, Paper, Scissors

The game of rock, paper, scissors depends
on the difference between mineral, weft, and forge
but only in imagination. In act, the game turns

through hands: flesh, pulse
and shadow's ventriloquisms,
as your open hand rises above my closed fist.

It is the same with eyes, watching
wider than language, a sharp cold wind
wrenches dry leaves from branches,

blinding the corner of dusk
where the town square is filled with ghosts
but no one speaks of it, much, the auction block

where once slaves were sold, the intersection
where a car plowed into protesters.
The language game depends on some common understanding:

a balled fist is a rock, an open hand paper, two fingers scissors,
so fragile the warp of vision,
shadows your hands cast along my arms,

not words but signs.
Maybe this time you've won.
But the game of rock, paper, scissors never really ends,

no clear stopping point, just exhaustion—
lithic, parchment, transverse physics of the cut,
friction's vectoral force and counter force.

Tear open the place where the words mark.
You say I speak in
a private language, coded,

impossible to reach,
an apatite translucency
of winter sky, and ghosts never left behind.

Ephebus

Ghosts are not gymnasts but former gymnasts are a kind of ghost:

For a while, mother and I lived in a hotel
off Gramercy Park, not the nice part.

I was in training
for surviving what came next. The mirror
in that small bathroom shaped a double self,
from which there's no complete recovery,
only shutting the heart.

Witness

One is not born but becomes a doll. The aftermath of
Civil Rights gave America dolls of variable shades
but never saved the daughters in this country.

The skin of a doll's manufactured from dye, anilines.
In a drugstore, once, I chose a dark-eyed doll
with black hair and buckskin gown,

grandmother bought it for my gift.
Back home, grandfather called it *filth*.
In grandmother's sewing room, the doll was then kept

deep inside the thread closet, where I often hid.
A thousand brilliant colors on spools,
where souls could be mended in secret.

Pretty Little Dolls

In the taxi at Michaelmas,
he wraps his arm to my waist.
I flinch the way dolls freeze.
September's fulgurance, a golden drought
shimmers the river trees we pass.

I once was a physician of souls.
My patients were pretty little dolls,
wrapped in bright packaging,
sold in stores with shining, honed faces.

Mother pays even now to save face.
I pull myself to the corner of his car.
This day of atonement and of rents due,
of bringing crimes before the Lord's judgment.

Photographs of Daughters

Mother touches our hair before the flash, her fingers wet with spit.
The backyard playground equipment's already rusted
fragile, friable paint. Behind the house, a fence
where the neighbor often leans
smoking cigarettes, watching us play.

Small daughters in photographs,
wearing red dresses as autumn leans toward us,
closing the doors of the house against cold.
In such photographs, it's not raining outside.
But the wind's high. Take a red car
out of town, don't return to the picture.

Carnal

Fold into metal boxes the unlatched Ferris wheel;
perimeter rain recedes into fields.
Up the ladder of the tilt-a-wheel climb.
Unhinge each joist, shut
the structure for travel.

The strippers in tents put on their clothes,
their morning voices the voices of ghosts.
You can't take it off like that
and not be wounded, working rough.
The girls drink Nyquil afterwards
to soothe, bottles of the stuff.

I'd like to walk away from this shore,
from all I know of ocean,
benthic depth and press, pelagic
cornerless rooms. A motherless place.
Whoever says the ocean is our mother
never saw a man drown. In ocean's crosswinds,

kneel ash and pine. The distance between
sky and land narrows,
horizon where vision happens:
even the men watching
naked girls dance for cash
know the eye alone is human.

Put away the giant slide, rides of grace
and penitence, saints outlasting faith.
Children run up the hill from water,
as men smoking cigarettes dangle on ladders
taking it all down, unshriven machines
carried by boxcar to the next town.

Doll Photographer

Not every form that has body has soul.
Consider the noetic eyes of the doll.

In the back room of a borrowed house, no furniture
except an old chest of drawers and mattress.

A storm's pulling in from the west.

I grew up on America's back roads, the scent of gasoline
leaching into the human cab.

Anaphora. Repeat the exercise.

With my noetic eyes, I spy
a desolate America, watch

gold light in the hotel room, horizon line
between sky and water,

endlessly opening. Stretch
my eyes for the distance.
This world will be destroyed for an illusion.

HUMAN

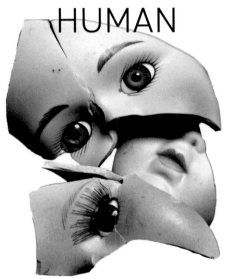

Unwearyingly with energies not their own.
—Maria Rainer Rilke

What Little Girls Learn

Once I drove a car to the fields past the town, ran out of gas.
I got out and walked. Thirty years later, still walking
at the border of dusk
because I cannot tell lies.

What little girls learn:
Be pretty, show cleavage once you have it.
Be polite, don't argue for your own sake.
Smoke cigarettes in private.
It's the softest way to kill yourself
without having to take responsibility for death.

Don't complain about your father's love
that goes too far, or your mother's acquiescence.
Learn to acquiesce yourself.
Learn to kneel, open your voice
as collateral wreckage.

The car stalled and there was nothing for it, empty tank.
Just wait 'til someone came by, take my chances.
I am from this country.

Anatomically Correct

You know it's a cheap hotel but have no better option.
Cut your hair carelessly and look like hell,
even so, at least you can see now all the way through,
looking down a hallway to a mirror
where the noun becomes a verb.

A city only half painted, a half open door.
A doll anatomically correct
is grotesque, the worst.
It's called the uncanny gap.

You know the place is cheap but tolerate it
allowing him to smoke, toss the ashes.
Childhood always ends in wreckage
of one or another sort, hence
in New Haven taught yourself to play the piano
in a small room where none could hear that private music.

And Deborah gave you an amulet
a scarab of lapis lazuli, saying if you have to go home,
take this with you, her hands on your hair
like a saint. Edge of the city, Saint Vincent's hospital,

traffic's oceanic curve. Don't go inside, or she'll never return.

Movies About Solitary Confinement

Movies about solitary confinement must be
unspeakably boring, and also tragic. Somehow
the only room they found for me
was solitary confinement, wherein I turned 15.

Years later, we were half asleep in a hotel after a storm,
and the woman cleaning
our room moved so carefully around us
I knew something bad must've happened to her,

sometime, but I don't think she was ever in solitary.
Her hands were too steady.
I don't smoke any more
but still dream about it, ashes flickering

metallic and angelic, catching flight.
To make someone else's bed
takes extreme tenderness
or desperation. She worked around us,

pretending not to see.
As if we were actually holy.
From warming seas, waters rise.

Shore grass black with flood's receding depth.

After Ballet

She picks me up in the blue Chevrolet, full of night sky.

Evangelists, certain of their own salvation, lose the way. Dark
and clean,

this pure shadow of travel, the car's rusted and we ride
eating bread, bitter rye,

morsels of survival. After ballet, the world is made
of straws of night. She arrives.

Across the parking lot other cars turn to stone, obfusc. She
throws me the keys.

Not yet fourteen, I drive
to the grocery. We buy apples for supper.

The positions of ballet are fixed and formal
and of whole numbers—first, second, third, fourth, fifth.

In the car, we eat red fruit, windows open,
our table of the vanishing point.
Spit out the glistening seeds.

House for Book

At age 16, I couldn't bear to do laundry.
Each night, shed my garments onto a narrow bed,
leaving them as if they were a dead girl's clothes.
Outfit by outfit, night after day, until I had nothing left
to wear and nowhere to sleep

as the clothes filled the mattress like a door in a frame.
Sometimes, chose a boy for a bed
to sleep in, his clothes
I'd put on in the morning,
and he'd stare, *you look strange in my sweater.*

I survived, adding like to like. Adjunction.
Add to this set already containing moths,
some billboards, and shabby but not fully ruined
hotels. And include also my narrow,
late childhood bed.

Some Dolls

Some girls, when young, seem like dolls.
Everyone wants them, but there's no destination,
other than throwing the doll away at some point.

Some girls, when young, are prizes.
And then suddenly not.
A series of steps, derivatives of rain
without protection, insomnia comes in

crossing the bridge like a missing person
whose face haunts your memory, you keep seeing
the poster where you held onto the subway belt,
her eyes in your eyes.

Dolls are made to be discarded.
A restaurant beneath the apartment kept open all night,
we could hear the easing and rising of rain,
men's hands touching their pockets.

As a doll, I was haunted by where men had touched me,
and wanted to speak of it. One can never prove anguish.

I washed the sink reiteratively at that window
where the bridge entered
through reflection,
in gusts of sky.

Cupboard

Of doll-like, silent intent
is hunger's ghostlier
language, gauge

of breath: *et spiritus sancti.*
A house is sky folded
back. I return. I am what comes back.

Further and further down
pinewoods' blood horizon,
her cupboard offered:

canned peaches, jars of peas, empty
lunchboxes, childhood's lead-soldered remnants.
Wind crossing dead winter grass.

Union Station, Washington, D.C.

We're all waiting. Even the women who carry
like sheathes of winter wheat
their belongings in plastic bags
must attend to what comes next. Pigeons coast

rafters, iridescent-throated rock-doves.
Green screens flicker with arrivals, delays,
departures. Awaiting
a stillness to calm the mind.

The man who's found in the trash
a clock radio, with batteries still intact, turns it on.
The clock he's salvaged no longer tracks time.
But it plays music louder than boarding announcements.

He curls to the clock radio, smiling,
as if recognizing his mother's voice.
We gather in the station's linear hollow. She rests
now, closing her eyes, the woman whose life is tied

in ten plastic bags, fanning around her feet
like children with wide-open, violet eyes.

Rust

My mother had no sons, none
to save her from her husband. She dreamed of a boy,
naming the family dogs Ralph, Roger,
Daniel, Zacharias, Jeff—

the animals could hardly shoulder it, being simple beasts.
Rust ate our playground equipment,
our swing-sets sounding minor keys,
pressed back and forth across rain's ache.

She'd hand me a scythe: *Cut the grass.*
Father would neglect the yard for months
and I was the strongest of her daughters.
I could cut grass, swing the scythe. But she dreamed of sons

with soft eyes, and calloused hands, driving fast at dusk.
I alone swept the leaves from the veranda, down and out, without
a boy to carry her voice, transmute
the house from tarnish.

Rust swallows metal: by the rail line
my mother is walking,
pacing herself to its template.
Coming home to it.

Princess Bed

No princess ever slept in a princess bed.
Even so, mother drove to Burlington, North Carolina,
a warehouse back door where a man leaning close
to her forehead said, *yes*

I should inhabit a princess
bedroom suite. She pulled it off
turning her face, barter
of course, what a pretty daughter. Princess,

if you awaken in terror for the world,
meditate, put away
your knowledge of petrochemical plastic factories,
fossil fuel combustion, franchises soldering lead.

Princess bed: pale cream
lacquer trimmed with faux gold,
cinematic vesture, fake
salvation's gilded signature.

Princess Coat

A wound that looks like a pretty dress.
When small, I always won the schoolyard footrace
desperate for any way out.

Put on the coat, button up where it hurts.
Tobacco breathes in fields under a late frost.
Used to run so far into it, bright and dark arrows, leaves
unsheltering and of time's smoke.

Sky muscles through its bones of breath
against collared earth, shadow salvage.
Salvage is the kindest word for what's lost.
Find it again. Not the same house
but another, a strange woman at the door,
her dark hair like smoke.

I curse myself for listening to a vanishing grief
but the princess coat is cut formally
indented sharp at the waist, readily

caught by men's hands.
Be the favorite daughter again.
The one who is not a tree or a river but a psalm.
A bridegroom coming out of his chamber . . .

Tobacco burdens earth with its rust verdigris.
Salvation is not salvage,
like the daughter in the belly of the wolf.
How long night lasts
after they've stripped you.

Childhood Plays

Lush theater in a dark terrain,
we were children with bread in our pockets,
with carefully folded hands,
pressed shirts and dresses, and
oh, with buttered bread in pockets.

After the play, it's a long walk
through heavy rains.
Lush theater, forest-dark.
Eustacy swells the ocean, drives the storms.
We learn the words by heart.

Hostel Girls

They're not mean, just trapped.
Bougainvillea shadow their rooms,
rented for a few dollars a day.
A narrow path, along which scrub

jays and men's footsteps stutter.
Hostel beds go cheap,
a place to put your stash.
These girls, they're not cruel just caught,

sleeping on cots, eating candy for supper.
Opalescent lacquer of dusk
gleams the hostel's rowed windows.
The girls aren't hostile, nor beggars. But waiting, waiting.

Cloister

Mother never owned a piano, she borrowed
the instrument from others, osculant,
feeding her daughters apples

from orchards drenched in pesticides.
Twelve-petalled rose,
I don't sleep well, these nights, just keep awake listening.

Twelve-petalled rose, twelve turns.
Along wet grass, insects
drag their shadows:

twelve petals of the rose,
polar functions,
the sound of night waits in you,

apples slightly past their prime,
the look of eyes bruised
from days-long exhaustion.

The Doll I Was

A magazine article about the rise in popularity of sex dolls
listed the measurements of a standard-issue model.
With a chill I saw they were almost my own
measurements, only my bust smaller by an inch or so.

The article delicately failed to imbue these dolls
with the illusion of minds or souls.
The leisure section article noted that buyers' peccadillos
could be met by special orders: dolls Rubenesque,

buck-toothed, or short as a child. Any quirk.
Skin color, eyes, hair. All up for grabs.
In my father's house, it never went well for me,
books unread on a dark shelf. Up for grabs—

like tripping and falling, between
grandmother teaching me to read at age three
and the next forty years as I learned
to skirt his shadow.

Like movies after the chase scene,
when it's alright you can breathe now.
This inch less.

Night Insects

I was raised in a house of quiet criminals,
elegantly getting away with it.
Insects crawled the counter,
brushed off, yes, but not harmless.

The English language is a bastard tongue.
What's it from, really? Germanic, Latinate, Brythonic.
The insect crawls at night
from my parents' room,

where he's never caught
but grows old and moves away
into smaller, more opulent apartments.
I grew up in a house of devout criminals,

drinking from lead crystal.
In such decanters, lead adheres to liquid,
molecules bringing to the drinker's blood
a slowness like frostbite.

You'll never entirely recover yourself.
Insects traverse the boundary
back and forth,
bad dreams of history.

Action Figure Toys

The compactness of their forms belies
how infinitely they coast.
You can lose them, like any material object,
in red earth at the limits of house.

Childhood's best toy vanishes.
Someone digs it up years later—
grit in its eyes, for its pillow a small stone.
Action figures survive oftentimes

in pieces, a hand here, there a coat of *maille*
fashioned in shining vintage plastic.
I'd run a mile, turn back, find myself
by thick tongues of magnolia, frangipani

shimmering through light. Not a daughter
but an action figure, surviving
the palaces of dirt at palings.
Most skilled at falling and surviving,

they haunt the edges
of backyards, returning
to a laden center where magnolia leans
heavily into morning shadows.

Like middle school rumors, they persist.
Pressed into service, action figures

accrue beneath surface gravel.
Fold into that horizon also

a vision of my late aunt, chain-smoking
all night above the kitchen sink, snuffing
the flame at first light,
embers scintillating against scrubbed steel.

Superhero Costume,
Attic, Tifton, Georgia

Superhero costume of my attic insomnia
delicately of polyester is woven.
The world is deep and tired and frayed,
wanting to sleep but remembering too bad dreams.

Superhero costume from childhood
the fabric worn thin, design still legible
web of childhood—

begin again with attic's colloquium
of dark birds and mirrors
left behind from the human world

begin again for silence and fields merge
forest and opalescent dialogues converge
and the attic holds its stopped worlds
history, milk, of frangipani and dark oratory roses.

The costume fit me oddly, being a woman not a boy
even so I am a person with a body and put on the garment,
polyvalent tension,

summer in the attic's dark hill—
put on the costume, make it work, fill the metamorphosis
for it was always going to end, indifferent

to time, the superhero flies above it
or is tragically altered and made new.

Earth waits in the foyer
mending an Orphic stain.

Becoming a Doll

To become a doll cannot happen by choice. It has to be forced.
Put on heavy make-up. Silence your thoughts.

Flanging the house, willows in hot winds bend.
Honeysuckle gulch

glittering synesthetic. Stay out of the house
where your mother is sleeping all day,

unable to awaken and face the history
that with you she inherits.

Peacock Coat

Every year she gives me the same coat
that does not fit. Resplendent peacock,
raw silk stitched on the bias.
I cut myself to its contours,

filigree of rust along selvedge,
felted edges trimmed away, eroded.
I wear this mirror-backing,
canted weft of rain.

Every year, the same gift, that cannot fit,
as winter sun disappears, silt
eluvium, along a blue horizon.
She brings me the coat

lined with a thousand invisible scars.
I know and do not know
it will always be given,
coat of holiness and killing style,

each year opening the box like a child.
Behind the house, feral peacocks cry like it's all lost.

She gives me the coat to which I've been cut.
My hunger stitched into the stuff.

The Insect Doll

Insects on leaves – willow, wisteria, hydrangea –
Not as individuals but *en masse*
insects will surpass us.
Winter will end completely.

There will be no winter left.
The insects will rise
from slotted secret warmth of house,
exoskeleton, thorax, petiole,

sensing any opening, however narrow.
These gaps of survival,
thread between buried
weather and the quick of the house.

Anagrammatic swerve, the insect doll
never waits for him to ask forgiveness.

The Incest Doll

I want one space pure, left over
from all the vast memorial cloth
of televisions, phones, computers screens. One place

without connection, only rain,
minding empty fields bordered by sumac,
a herd of bucks, antlers frozen with grief.

Tried to pretend those motels were *nice*
but the dirtiness of pretense doesn't fix.
Dusk begins at the ridge, rises from bedrock hematite.

At the field's limit, sumac carries red sky.
I tried to move on, forget the whole event.
But the rains remembered
those hallways where I abandoned you.

Manikin

The vestments of the manikin alter easily enough.
But she herself never changes, body of vinyl,
that once was beautiful.
I took my mother's wallet
with her permission, on condition
that I pledge silence about what happened.

A manikin garners neither wage nor voice
but occupies space and time, distance
ravels in its hypaethral mind.
The fourth dimension
isn't time or light or gravity, but memory.

Every strip mall's haunted, awaiting a voice,
make the table dance. At the junction
of Covington and Conyers, trains are long gone.

Where the train line breaks into forest
we got out and walked, coats held above our heads
to hold off drowning time.

Antique Doll

In unsettled hotels, places once fine, admonitory antique dolls,
propped in baskets of azure and red-lead.

Mother fed us small cups like cuts,
practicing our recitals of silence.

Lug our stuff up the worn stairs, recurrent,
the same scuffed carpet, shabby rooms of genteel persistence.

In dawn's indigo stir I dream she offers a clean shirt
the color of new sky, and says *Come on, we'll get out of here,*

shed this bad dream of ancestry.
Antique dolls. Feral ghosts.

Doll Daughter

I will feed her ambrosia from a bottle so small
she won't need to open her mouth.
Keep her immaculate, don't let her ever hear the word *whore*.

He says *calm down,*
but there's no reason to be calm.
A house going to seed,
black flashing ocean along shore rocks.

Next door, terns rise. Valedictory strays.
Their shadows fall like bruises.
I set her in a basket of glass rain
in a widow's walk, left over
from the era of homecomings.

Growing Up Skipper

for Amy and Victoria

In a plastic world, they carry the human
form without mind, lips parted
by what cannot be told and must be said,

bearing on narrow shoulders the melancholy
stir of childhood afternoons in playrooms
of richer daughters. Battle

for such thin ascendancy—whose Barbie
cost more, purchased newer, which doll owns
better clothes, furniture, car, boudoir. A horse.

I played understanding the world was ending,
willing to steal from blessèd girls
with a sleight of hand so delicate

for years I got away with it until, aged 13,
the past caught up with me, my own form shifting
like the stolen goods in my closet.

Dolls with pop-out breasts, of vinyl parts, comport
without measurable intelligence. Yet they know
the cost. To become a woman

takes only a twist of the arm
and, *legerdemain,* you're changed.
Now these slate late afternoons return—

plastic forms love cannot mend.
So much more than I took
has been taken from me.

Dress Like A Girl

We drove out to Moultrie to buy a dress
to wear to the funeral. Behind pine trees,
the sky flagrant bright, back-lit, glossy.
The seamstress said I was a doll
standing so still and useless, eyes glazed.

Thunderstorm hit on the way back.
In her kitchen, centuries of rain
weighed the windows down,
loblolly and longleaf pine swept to earth,
red needles marking air with rust.
A thousand years of rain under the magnolia roots.

The dead we buried. Up all night afterwards,
so brightly awake, preparing our suitcases,
our next-day garments.

City of Disappeared Girls

In memoriam Morgan, Yeardley, Sage, and Hannah

I live in a city that tries to forget
daughters who left but never meant to.
In my city, shadows leach from statues.
Waking dreams haunted by vertigo,

I too have been mistaken
for one who can be made to bend.
I live in a city of starlings and dogwood
Statues stare through stone eyes.

About the dead, I have no right to speak.
But this is my city and I live here, paying rent.
Tenting black oaks, starlings cross.
As much as anyone, I want to reverse
that bridge of the falling sun,
the burning word, *return*.

It will only hurt for a minute
step along the bridge whitened with rain.
Everyone takes advantage, but I come back
to the house of limits
because all equations balance
but some reach insolvable forms.

About the dead, I will not speak, only
of those gone and not done.
City of lost girls. Statues watch

from plinths of trash; smoke the cigarette
and confess the story.

It's almost night, almost midwinter.
Joan sends a photograph, a solstice prayer.

The Puppet King

For some, puppetry is an art, for others a condition.
My father pulled the strings.
I'd get undressed to see myself,
to understand, I am only an image.

A puppet, a doll, and a photograph
share the common thread
of mirrors' exactitude.

For some, puppetry is a gift, a performance.
But for those within the play it's serious
and nothing to do with craft.

Shadow puppets all my infancy hung
above the boundary chairs,
shedding leaded paint flakes,

shadows' material veer.
For those watching,
the puppet play Is simple,

like maps of fields that move through sky.
But for those inside,
good and evil divide

along the fretted line of friable leaded paint.
The puppet's art is all
about pain, enduring, saying nothing
except what is spoken through you,

like light turns through wheeling leaves.
How it feels to be a puppet—
to long for your own hands, voice
but once released you cannot get the hang of it.

Without his pull, you flatten,
the music of mirrors so hard to hear,
then suddenly the show's alight,
with a wound that feels like words.

My father thought he pulled
the strings, above it all,
collector, ethnographer.
But he too was behind the screen,
Ravana, the demon king.

Doll Mother

Silence is a doll's cede.
With her lacquer-polished hair, she was always
more beautiful than her daughters.

The night watchman of the apartments loves her, she is sure.
Under his hand, she holds still as frozen earth,
steadied in the entrance-hall chair. At night, deep into the dark,
she tallies what her girls had cost her,
the damages she saw when turning to the mirror,
even the night watchman's hands could not heal.

She's jealous of love. Her looks won't fail
but they'll set hard, in the manner of dolls,
the kind left propped up in apartment complex halls,
grown daughters moved on to school or marriage or simply open air.
She stays here: graying carpets smelling sweetly of closeted garbage,
the passage grown tawdry by trammeling and vacuuming.

She wants her girls to feel what she felt, the fall
of porcelain under a man's hand, shelved for years
without testimony, reflecting on nothing
but the quiet stairway landing.

She doesn't want the neighbors to learn
how she gave them up, each in turn,
because they drained her milk and her teeth began to falter.
She casts no blame on any man.
Her mouth never moves, just a toying half-smile,
doll-hungry, a few pearl dots exposed.

Rabbit Theory

In the year of plague, from depth of backyard gulch, rabbits emerge,
ablative, separate from the human world
but visible to us. A shared visibility between human and rabbit.

One evening, for a walk in the yard, I opened
the back door to see a rabbit crouched beneath the nearest tree,
frozen at the sound of me. *Wait,* I told myself, *wait*
until the creature moves away, —

the rabbit held still until I stepped out,
to gain the yard as my domain, mortgaged.
The creature bolted, crossing
my path near as breath, leaving the yard bereft.

The theory of rabbit. Don't. Don't insist.
For the dining-room table where my parents
once served esteemed university professors,
colleagues of my fathers in the deep South,
stands now in my basement. Not far from the rabbits' more secret house.

Now the table rests, empty of guests,
and the once famous, buried and forgotten, persist
only in my night terrors, waking, remembering
unwanted touch, listening

for the rabbit's silence. The backyard lush and unkempt
in the plague year. For such grace of ground.

The rabbits have their secret mirror into which even they never
gaze, too holy,
for human tables. Crepuscular feeders, initiates.
On such narrow shoulders the rabbit carries us.

Bright Shoes

No words without shadows. Consider *vulnerable,*
easily wounded. Shopping malls,
closing down across the country,
leave vacant parking lots like dark hallways.

In a shopping mall on the brink, ten years ago,
my father purchased bright shoes
for my son, a waning August evening.
My son was four years old, and the decorated shoes

flickered with mercuric light at each step.
Because of my father, I still wake up
bad nights, crying *get off me!*
hitting at sky.

Shopping malls, built primarily in the 1970s,
stood to kill space and time.
The mall of my childhood was built in the shape of a cross
like a Jesuit meditation.

In new shoes, the child ran fast
up and down the aisles, lit and unlit,
dusk sky shimmering at glass doorways.
In this parable

of my father's love there is neither good
nor evil, only wound. *Vulnerable.*

How proud the boy was of his shoes,
and of his grandfather.

What I could not allow him to hold.
We caught the last bus out of town, one seat,
I held him in my lap, the shoes flickering
like ghosts or angels, whichever steps we take.

.

ABOUT THE POET

PHOTO: Amy Wilton

CLAIRE MILLIKIN'S poetry has appeared in numerous literary journals and magazines. She is the author of the poetry collections *Ransom Street* (2019), *State Fair Animals* (2018), *Tartessos and Other Cities* (2016), *Television* (2016), *After Houses* (2014), *Motels Where We Lived* (2014), and *Museum Of Snow* (2013). She received her BA in philosophy from Yale University, MFA in poetry from New York University, and PhD in English literature from the Graduate Center of the City University of New York. Millikin teaches at the University of Maine. http://claire-raymond.org. ∎

OTHER BOOKS BY 2LEAF PRESS

2Leaf Press challenges the status quo by publishing alternative fiction, non-fiction, poetry and bilingual works by activists, academics, poets and authors dedicated to diversity and social justice with scholarship that is accessible to the general public. 2Leaf Press produces high quality and beautifully produced hardcover, paperback and ebook formats through our series: *2LP Explorations in Diversity, 2LP University Books, 2LP Classics, 2LP Translations, Nuyorican World Series,* and *2LP Current Affairs, Culture & Politics.* Below is a selection of 2Leaf Press' published titles.

2LP EXPLORATIONS IN DIVERSITY
Substance of Fire: Gender and Race in the College Classroom
by Claire Millikin
Foreword by R. Joseph Rodríguez, Afterword by Richard Delgado
Contributed material by Riley Blanks, Blake Calhoun, Rox Trujillo

Black Lives Have Always Mattered
A Collection of Essays, Poems, and Personal Narratives
Edited by Abiodun Oyewole

The Beiging of America:
Personal Narratives about Being Mixed Race in the 21st Century
Edited by Cathy J. Schlund-Vials, Sean Frederick Forbes, Tara Betts
with an Afterword by Heidi Durrow

What Does it Mean to be White in America?
Breaking the White Code of Silence, A Collection of Personal Narratives
Edited by Gabrielle David and Sean Frederick Forbes
Introduction by Debby Irving and Afterword by Tara Betts

2LP CLASSICS
Adventures in Black and White
Edited and with a critical introduction by Tara Betts
by Philippa Duke Schuyler

Monsters: Mary Shelley's Frankenstein and Mathilda
by Mary Shelley, edited by Claire Millikin Raymond

2LP TRANSLATIONS
Birds on the Kiswar Tree
by Odi Gonzales, Translated by Lynn Levin
Bilingual: English/Spanish

Incessant Beauty, A Bilingual Anthology
by Ana Rossetti, Edited and Translated by Carmela Ferradáns
Bilingual: English/Spanish

NUYORICAN WORLD SERIES
Our Nuyorican Thing, The Birth of a Self-Made Identity
by Samuel Carrion Diaz, with an Introduction by Urayoán Noel
Bilingual: English/Spanish

Hey Yo! Yo Soy!, 40 Years of Nuyorican Street Poetry,
The Collected Works of Jesús Papoleto Meléndez
Bilingual: English/Spanish

LITERARY NONFICTION
No Vacancy; Homeless Women in Paradise
by Michael Reid

The Beauty of Being, A Collection of Fables, Short Stories & Essays
by Abiodun Oyewole

TRAVELOGUE
The Wanderer
by Carole J. Garrison

WHEREABOUTS: Stepping Out of Place,
An Outside in Literary & Travel Magazine Anthology
Edited by Brandi Dawn Henderson

PLAYS
Rivers of Women, The Play
by Shirley Bradley LeFlore, with photographs by Michael J. Bracey

AUTOBIOGRAPHIES/MEMOIRS/BIOGRAPHIES
Trailblazers, Black Women Who Helped Make America Great
American Firsts/American Icons (Volumes 1-3)
by Gabrielle David

Mother of Orphans
The True and Curious Story of Irish Alice, A Colored Man's Widow
by Dedria Humphries Barker

Strength of Soul
by Naomi Raquel Enright

Dream of the Water Children:
Memory and Mourning in the Black Pacific
by Fredrick D. Kakinami Cloyd
Foreword by Velina Hasu Houston, Introduction by Gerald Horne
Edited by Karen Chau

The Fourth Moment: Journeys from the Known to the Unknown, A Memoir
by Carole J. Garrison, Introduction by Sarah Willis

POETRY

PAPOLÍTICO, Poems of a Political Persuasion
by Jesús Papoleto Meléndez
with an Introduction by Joel Kovel and DeeDee Halleck

Critics of Mystery Marvel, Collected Poems
by Youssef Alaoui, with an Introduction by Laila Halaby

shrimp
by jason vasser-elong, with an Introduction by Michael Castro
The Revlon Slough, New and Selected Poems
by Ray DiZazzo, with an Introduction by Claire Millikin

A Country Without Borders: Poems and Stories of Kashmir
by Lalita Pandit Hogan, with an Introduction by Frederick Luis Aldama

Branches of the Tree of Life
The Collected Poems of Abiodun Oyewole 1969-2013
by Abiodun Oyewole, edited by Gabrielle David
with an Introduction by Betty J. Dopson

FLORIDA | NEW YORK
www.2leafpress.org